Quotes and *Confirmations*

"EVERYTHING YOU NEED TO HEAR TO LIVE AN INSPIRED AND PURPOSEFUL LIFE"

2nd Edition

BEYOND WYNN

Can the coach count on you to do your best every day that he puts you in the game?

■ ■ ■

If the coach came to you and said, "Do you want me to take you out of the game?" what would you say?

■ ■ ■

If you cheat your finances, they will leave you.

■ ■ ■

You get better after you get hit.

■ ■ ■

Coach put us all in the game together for a reason.

When coach retires your jersey, there's NO getting back in.

■ ■ ■

Make an appointment with yourself today.

■ ■ ■

If you're not where you want to be in your life, change your routines and activities.

■ ■ ■

In order to get rich quick, you have to change today.

■ ■ ■

Focus on the relationships, the money will follow.

The more you work on your personal development, the easier your life will be.

■ ■ ■

If you try to skip self-development, your life will be rough.

■ ■ ■

It doesn't make sense/cents teaming up to lose.

■ ■ ■

Most of us struggle because we're looking for a microwave solution.

■ ■ ■

Too many expenses will make your eyes look like oil base paint. LOL

You ever talk to someone on the phone that used to have money and they sound totally different? LOL

■ ■ ■

Babies remind us that we don't need money in order to smile.

■ ■ ■

The more you follow and trust your vision, the better you will feel.

■ ■ ■

God's plan for us is for us to leave our gifts here on earth, not die with them.

■ ■ ■

God shows us the way every day; we choose to ignore our built-in GPS.

Building relationships is the best strategy for long term success.

■ ■ ■

Marry the process and great results will follow.

■ ■ ■

Perform miracles and expect miracles.

■ ■ ■

Your dreams don't care if you feel like it; trust me, they know somebody that does.
LOL

■ ■ ■

If the room is dark, you cut the light on. If you don't like where you are in life, you demonstrate your genius.

What if you were required to demonstrate your genius in exchange for air? LOL

■ ■ ■

God hired us to create win-wins, so don't get fired. LOL

■ ■ ■

Faith is the cure for most illusions, with no side-effects.

■ ■ ■

The babies are trying to save us from extinction, but we refuse to listen.

■ ■ ■

Babies are a gift from God and a sign/ opportunity for us to change this crash course.

Death told me to live while I can.

■ ■ ■

God didn't give you the gift of life to be worried about death. Go live.

■ ■ ■

You can't live your best life afraid and dodging pain.

■ ■ ■

The life that you crave thrives on the other side of fear.

■ ■ ■

Adults say kids are the future, but they also say if they only knew earlier what they know now.

Sometimes you just got to pack up and move to an island. LOL

■ ■ ■

Your dream isn't scared of you, so why are you scared of it?

■ ■ ■

Money will always be attracted to the person that gives it the most attention.

■ ■ ■

Don't hide your story—somebody needs it.

■ ■ ■

Rough stories sell the best; you may be on to something.

God is calling but you won't pick up.

■ ■ ■

Has God ever told you, "You only call me when you need something"?

■ ■ ■

I imagine all of us winning.

■ ■ ■

Investing in real estate can fund your dreams.

■ ■ ■

Being yourself will energize you. Trying to fit in will drain your energy.

Is your Christmas gift still under the tree?
God gave you an amazing gift; unwrap that
one too.

■ ■ ■

Not using your gift is like not wearing your
winter coat in ten degree weather.

■ ■ ■

That person that you admire had to
graduate from where you are today.

■ ■ ■

Success and excuses can't live together,
somebody has to move out.

■ ■ ■

I'll get worried when everyone moves out of
their homes and starts living in cars.

God gave us all the ability to make this world a better place. Are you participating?

■ ■ ■

If you were money, would you stay with you?

■ ■ ■

Don't tell me the answer, show me.

■ ■ ■

The love of people is the root of longevity for all humanity.

■ ■ ■

Your vision is waiting on you to demonstrate.

The things that we grow through can make us rich if we don't give up.

■ ■ ■

The things that we overcome can be used to comfort others on their journey

■ ■ ■

God didn't give you that gift and say, "Wait until Monday, Friday, the first of the month, New Year or income tax season."

■ ■ ■

Create your recipe to change your life.

■ ■ ■

The book won't help if you don't act.

We all have what it takes, but only a few demonstrate it.

■ ■ ■

Most people struggle because they're not impeccable with their word.

■ ■ ■

Personal credit can change your bank account, business and your life.

■ ■ ■

Your word is the key to your success.

■ ■ ■

Great relationships are life-changing; be intentional.

If you became good friends with fear, what could stop you?

■ ■ ■

Don't allow your bank account to dictate your energy.

■ ■ ■

I arrested my development, not the police.

■ ■ ■

The judge is doing his job, I'm not doing mine.

■ ■ ■

If you don't manage yourself, time won't matter.

Death has taught me what no man can teach.

■ ■ ■

Death is a great teacher, pay attention.

■ ■ ■

Pause... are you excited about your journey so far? If not, change the station.

■ ■ ■

Your life is like a television; you can tune in to whatever station you like.

■ ■ ■

If you owed God the money, would you pay it back?

Go on a tour with yourself—inside.

■ ■ ■

Trusting God makes sense/cents.

■ ■ ■

Death teaches great love lessons.

■ ■ ■

Death can make you speed up.

■ ■ ■

God didn't put your gift in somebody else's hands.

You want to find the key to success, explore yourself.

■ ■ ■

Don't die to live.

■ ■ ■

Help before you need help, and you'll always have help.

■ ■ ■

Sometimes all you need to know is what doesn't work.

■ ■ ■

You'll pay to cut the line at the club, but you don't see the value in paying a coach to cut your learning curve.

People love results but hate the process.

■ ■ ■

If you want to be successful, go start making mistakes today. LOL

■ ■ ■

If you love money, act like it.

■ ■ ■

Don't read another book until you apply something from the last book you've read.

■ ■ ■

I paid to upload what's in my brain. If you want to download something, you have to pay to pick my brain.

How would you like to be remembered?
Start today.

■ ■ ■

You're paying a huge cost for not over standing the power of your subconscious mind.

■ ■ ■

You tell me what would happen if you recycled your money.

■ ■ ■

I'm motivated to help for a fee, not free. LOL

■ ■ ■

Your brain is worth more than you can imagine.

Cures don't create residual income, but sickness does.

■ ■ ■

If you use the gifts that God gave you, your life will be forever changed.

■ ■ ■

Take a look inside; what you really need is there.

■ ■ ■

If you stop trying to skip the process, your grass can look better than the country club's grass.

■ ■ ■

You own peace; stop paying for it.

Happiness is yours to keep.

■ ■ ■

You should own the rights to your own happiness.

■ ■ ■

Happy and sad is the menu; what are you choosing?

■ ■ ■

If you show up, the results will find you.

■ ■ ■

Accept and love yourself, the rest is easy.

You will never feel stressed out counting your blessings.

■ ■ ■

Happiness is the root of all real success.

■ ■ ■

Happy will attract things that sad can't.

■ ■ ■

The grass is greener because someone committed to the process.

■ ■ ■

If you've been given the wrong direction, you probably won't make it to your destination.

Go on a love spree—you can't overdose. LOL

■ ■ ■

Look at your neighbors and say, "I'm going to make coach proud of me."

■ ■ ■

Look up to God, not man.

■ ■ ■

God gave us the game. It's our responsibility to play ball.

■ ■ ■

God is trying to get in touch with you; pick up.

God gave you the GPS; trust it.

■ ■ ■

They over stand fake, they understand truth.

■ ■ ■

Life's menu... sad, happy lonely, great and okay.

■ ■ ■

I'm searching in, experimenting out.

■ ■ ■

We created the manual for the car, but fail to create a manual for the life we imagine.

Imagine the plane giving up every time it experienced turbulence. That's how God looks at you when you give up.

■ ■ ■

What coach gave us for free is better than anything that's on the market.

■ ■ ■

Coach gave us an unfair advantage.

■ ■ ■

You're fatigued because you're pretending to be something you're not. Be yourself.

■ ■ ■

The best vacation is free; travel inside yourself.

Ask yourself, "Does this make sense/cents?"

■ ■ ■

Get good at getting ideas off your mind, a.k.a., demonstrate.

■ ■ ■

What if the truth doesn't set you free? I'm not saying lie. LOL

■ ■ ■

Your mind is the best vehicle on the planet.

■ ■ ■

We would all get along perfect if we were blind.

For some strange reason we love each other more in a time of need.

■ ■ ■

If you're stressed because it's too noisy, cut it off.

■ ■ ■

Marry your money and have kids with it.

■ ■ ■

You should use your brain before it expires.

■ ■ ■

Coach didn't put you in the game to quit.

Nobody has it all together—be yourself.

■ ■ ■

You can choose one, so who will you listen to: God or people?

■ ■ ■

We're all the same size to God. You can keep those titles.

■ ■ ■

You have to grow for the life that you really want.

■ ■ ■

If God is your Daddy, what does that make you?

Your dream is probably in the idea that you didn't try.

■ ■ ■

Kids are now, not the future.

■ ■ ■

Have you ever seen a coach put a player in the game to help them lose?

■ ■ ■

Don't look for miracles, become one. God woke you up to help.

■ ■ ■

I heard they won't let you in heaven if you haven't used your gift.

The people that you admire unwrapped their gifts.

■ ■ ■

Be comfortable being naked, no matter what it looks like under there: Body/Life.

■ ■ ■

Relationships are KING.

■ ■ ■

Cut your light on and illuminate your gift.

■ ■ ■

If I cured you, would you come back?

We exist to inspire and be confirmation for each other.

■ ■ ■

Mama can't walk me through it, but she can talk me through it. I hear you loud and clear, Ma.

■ ■ ■

That idea is an opportunity. God gave you that idea for a reason.

■ ■ ■

Don't waste another idea. What if that idea was/is your gamechanger?

■ ■ ■

Would you care what he or she said if you were making $100K per month?

How many ideas do you have in storage? Don't lie. Your truth could help save a life.

■ ■ ■

Don't be stingy with your gifts. Are you happy with your motion picture?

■ ■ ■

If you knew your gift could create a legacy for your family, would you unwrap it?

■ ■ ■

The journey isn't even guaranteed, so be all you can be today.

■ ■ ■

If God said to you, "I'm retiring your jersey in twelve months," what three things would you do?

Everybody is looking for answers; sometimes it's the question that will change your life.

■ ■ ■

Your truth is multipurpose; it'll help you and others at the same time.

■ ■ ■

There's nothing you can do about the plane crashing, but you can do something about your negative bank account.

■ ■ ■

At some point, you have to take the seat belt off. Today.

■ ■ ■

If the coach pulled you out of the game today, would you be excited to watch your film?

Do something today you will be excited to watch when coach retires your jersey.

■ ■ ■

If you ever lost someone that you loved, raise your hand. Now imagine this: your loved one can't get back in the game, so it's up to you to take the team to the championship. Do you make excuses or BALL out of control?

■ ■ ■

Your gift is the answer that you've been looking for; unwrap it.

■ ■ ■

You can make millions or excuses but not both; think responsibly.

■ ■ ■

God is the only security.

Money is a great diversion.

■ ■ ▪

If you've learned the most from turbulence, why do you dodge anything that challenges you?

■ ■ ▪

There's a reason entertainment costs more than education—don't pay attention.

■ ■ ▪

Real Estate investing is too good to be true.

■ ■ ▪

I don't care what the cost is; you have a gift that will pay for it.

You can't live your best life dodging pain.

■ ■ ■

Fear will not allow you to thrive.

■ ■ ■

There's a reason God didn't want us to
share a brain.

■ ■ ■

No dreams, just goals powered by your
infinite intelligence and the mirror.

■ ■ ■

You can't grow wrong demonstrating your
genius.

If you know from experience that you've grown more from taking chances, take more chances. If you fall, God will catch you.

■ ■ ■

Sometimes it's the question that will change your life, not the answer.

■ ■ ■

You want to attract more money, be impeccable with your word.

■ ■ ■

Your dreams are going to need your full cooperation.

■ ■ ■

Imagine God putting your happiness in somebody else.

I can't give up, because I promised my vision
that I would see it through no matter what.

■ ■ ■

You own the work you put in.

■ ■ ■

God is your life jacket; jump.

■ ■ ■

Go beyond the physical; you'll be good.

■ ■ ■

If God is your safety net, what is it that you
can't do?

Successful people showed up somewhere consistently, and the results followed them.

■ ■ ■

It's possible to win at anything that you don't quit.

■ ■ ■

Give in, not up.

■ ■ ■

Your life will be hard as long as you continue to follow man and ignore God.

■ ■ ■

Your best life is an inside game, not outside.

The only thing you should be doing from the sidelines is cheering. If you want it done better, you do it.

■ ■ ■

Grow to your dreams. If you wait on them to come to your level, they may not make it.

■ ■ ■

Sometimes you must travel alone on this journey; embrace it.

■ ■ ■

Everyone believes in God until life gets tough.

■ ■ ■

God is trying to show you the way; listen in.

Made in the USA
Monee, IL
30 August 2020